Cloud Virginia Woodward, Reginald Bathurst

Down Durley Lane and other Ballads

Cloud Virginia Woodward, Reginald Bathurst

Down Durley Lane and other Ballads

ISBN/EAN: 9783744789080

Printed in Europe, USA, Canada, Australia, Japan

Cover: Foto ©Thomas Meinert / pixelio.de

More available books at **www.hansebooks.com**

Down Durley Lane
and Other Ballads

By
Virginia Woodward Cloud

With Illustrations by
Reginald B. Birch

New York : The Century Co. : 1898

To
My Mother

Contents.

Down Durley Lane

Down Durley Lane

OWN Durley Lane a-singing as I chanced for to go,
The brier was a-blossom, and the hedges were a-blow —
There I spied a piper, a-piping to the sky,
So down the lane and after him away went I.

" Oh, tell me, piper, tell me, why go you piping here ? "
" For honey-stalks and ox-lips and all the sweet o' year ! "

HERE the crooked turnstile at the
meadow stands
A brown and lithesome farmer lad was
whistling o'er his lands;
Only larks above the wheat could whistle
clear as he,
So through the meadow, after him, away
went we!

" Oh, tell us, farmer, tell us, why go you whistling gay ? "
" For barley-break and yellow moon and tossing of the hay ! "

OUT upon the highway from the nodding grass,
A-trilling of a silver song, we met a lovely lass;
She only smiled — I know not yet just how it did befall,
But up the highway, after her, away went we all!

" Oh, tell us, lovely, lovely lass, why go you singing there ? "
" Why, but for love-in-idleness, and dancing at the fair ! "

THERE, about a milestone, where the hill began,
    A-leaping and a-skipping we found the queerest man;
    He hopped and he laughed—'t was very strange to see,—
    So up the hill, and after him, away went we!

" Now, prythee, merry gentleman, why go you laughing, too ? "
" Forsooth, fair mates, because I fared this way, and
    met with you !"

ND lo, upon the hill-top, a mighty mistress gay,
Her satin petticoat was grand, her feathers fine were they!
Her buckles and her ribbons they flouted foot and head,
So, o'er the hill-top, after her, away we all sped!

"Oh, mistress, mighty mistress, what brings you o'er the lea?"
But she tossed her head right haughtily, and proudly
past minced she.

ND then, with pipe and singing, with laugh and whistle shrill,
The maddest music there was made a-dashing down the hill!
Until upon the green ways, nigh to Durley Fair,
We smiled at one another—and wondered we were there!

"*Now, why go we a-faring about the green ways here?*"
"*For such a blithesome company, and all the sweet o' year!*"

6

BUT why the Piper piped a tune so keenly strange and sweet,
And why the Farmer whistled so joyous through his wheat,
And what the magic meaning of the lovely lassie's song,
And why the queer man should leap so merrily along,

(And of that mighty mistress, who was so wondrous fine,—
With buckles peering through the dusk like fireflies a-shine),

WE never grew the wiser, nor learned what 't was about,
Although we danced upon the green until the
stars shone out;
And no one knows unto this day the how and
why and where—
Save that each followed someone else well-nigh
to Durley Fair.

Yet this, methinks, is very clear — in truth 't is
passing plain —
I tripped it once, when the world was gay, adown
green Durley Lane!

When Mistress Peggy comes to Town

WHEN MISTRESS PEGGY COMES TO TOWN

I.

THERE is such staring all about,
And such a running up and down;
The Dominie himself goes out,
And we behind him, two and two,—
We mind our manners, that we do,
When Mistress Peggy comes to town!

II.

The yellow coach goes rattling by,
With its white horses galloping;
The geese and chickens frightened fly,
Even the Parson's pigeons proud
Go scurrying through the dusty cloud;
The Blacksmith's anvil stops its ring!

III.

They draw up just a moment's
    space,
For water, at the "Trusty
    Three."
Once she leaned out,— we saw
    her face,—
It was so pink and sweet and
    all,
Like Granny's roses by the
    wall!
She smiled at Cicely and me.

IV.

Then toots the horn, the whip
    goes "crack!"
The dogs all bark the noise to
    drown,
And off they dash; the dust
    flies back;
The coach is out of sight at
    last.
You 'd think a wind-storm had
    blown past
When Mistress Peggy comes to
    town!

The Happy Holiday of Master Merrivein

The Happy Holiday of Master Merrivein

"I 'LL hie me up to Durley Fair," quoth Master Merrivein;
"A day of rest and jollity, then hie me home again.
With shillings in my pocket, and the harvest work all done,
I 'll spend a happy holiday, then back by set o' sun!"

So blithesome Master Merrivein, all in his Sun-
day best,
Started straightway for Durley Fair, with energy
and zest;
His stick upon his shoulder, most joyfully he
sped,
But suddenly a voice from a neighbor's gateway said:

"Oh, Master, Master Merrivein!
As you go to the fair,
Will you take my tumbler-pigeons to the
pigeon fakir there?"
So, kindly Master Merrivein, he slung
them on his back,
The pigeons and the pigeon-cage.
(They made a goodly pack!)

14

"HOLD! hold, there, Master Merrivein! As you go through the town,
    Will you leave this little donkey with brother Billy Brown?
    The donkey is so gentle, and so tractable,
        't is said,
That, if you do not beat him, he 'll just trot on ahead!"

So, kindly Master Merrivein, he added to his store,
By letting one small donkey just trot right on before.

"HO, there, you Master Merrivein! Go
    you by Durley Fair?
    Then please just take these candle-
    sticks to cousin Betty Blair!
    This bonnet, in the bonnet-box, I 'll add, if you don't mind,
    And these few little trifles I will just tie on behind!

    "They 're for my sister at the Inn, good sir; and
      mother begs
    To add this green umbrella and a basketful of eggs!"

So, kindly Master Merrivein, he took them on his arm,
For fear the bonnet and the eggs might straightway
    come to harm.

15

"H, Master, Master Merrivein! just step around this way!
If only you will drive a cow along with you to-day!
She's the gentlest, kindest animal that ever yet
was seen,
And I 've sold her to young Mistress Finch, who
lives on Durley Green!"

So, kindly Master Merrivein, he hummed a little song,
And the cow she switched her tail about and straightway went along.

"H, wait—wait, Master Merrivein! Please stop a moment where
The cross-roads meet the school-house, well-nigh to Durley Fair,
And give this keg of butter and bag of tarts so nice,
And this shawl and woolen comforter, to good old Granny Gryce!"

So, kindly Master Merrivein, with effort and
with care,
Got all these things slung on him,— no
matter how or where.

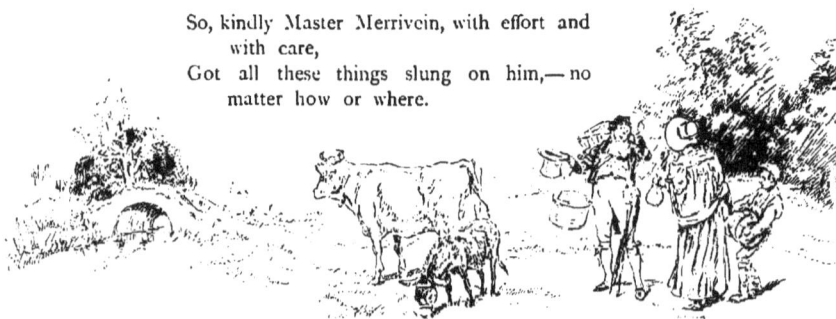

"Is that good Master Merrivein? Three squawking geese have I;
I 'll hang them on your shoulder, and their
  feet I 'll tightly tie.
Just leave them with Dame Blodgett, anear
  the crooked stile,
The other side of Durley Green, about a half
  a mile !"

"Oh, stop — stop,
  Master Merri-
  vein ! Go you
to Durley Fair?

Then I beg you take this finery for my
  daughter Meg to wear,
This flowered hat and tippet, the mitts and
  paduasoy.
She 's at Aunt Elsie's cottage, and will welcome you with joy !"

"Wait, there, good Master Merrivein ! If to
  the fair you go,
Please take my fiddle and my flute to
  Uncle Jerryjo !

The tuning-fork and music-rack, accordion
  and horn,
Are for his son, who leads the band at Durley
  Fair each morn !"

2

So, straightway, Master Merrivein, so good and true and kind,
Started him off to Durley Fair a day of rest to find.
But did he find it? Oh, dear me! Go ascertain, I pray,
Of all the curious country-folk who passed him on the way!

For the gentle little donkey,— that the sight you may not miss,
I 'll say it took an attitude occasionally like this,—

While the pigeons and the squawking geese,
I really am afraid,
That one small picture could not hold the
havoc that they made!

THE cow (that *gentle* animal!)—to-morrow, at the fair,
Young Mistress Finch may try to sell; I warn you, then
beware!
For Master Merrivein found out, to his own great surprise,
That she had an unexpected way of taking exercise.

AND all the other articles? Alack-a-day! I ween,
Some things, to be appreciated, really must be seen;
But if you'd fully understand the *how*, and *when*, and
where,
Go take a day (like Merrivein's) to rest at Durley Fair!

How the Dominie went to Sea

HOW THE DOMINIE WENT TO SEA

I'M going to see —" the Dominie said,
  With a nod of his gray, sagacious head
To a path that wound from the hill-
    side down
Away to a far-off seaport town —

"To see —" and he nodded, and off he went,
His hands behind and his wise head bent,
And a far-seeing look in his kind blue eyes
Fixed on some marvelous enterprise.

"To sea!" cried his wife from the trellised door.
"Was ever a man so queer before —
To start on a voyage as sudden as that,
In his every-day coat and his garden hat?

"Or ever a faithful, painstaking wife
As worried as I each day of my life,
To know what he may do next? Alack!
Dominie Brown, come back! Come back!"

But in vain she called, and in vain she ran;
The long-limbed Dominie, excellent man,
Was up the road that led to the hill,
Striding along with a right good will.

So the provident wife, who knew his ways,
Sped back, in a state of sore amaze,
For his three-cornered hat, and his long-tailed
    coat,
And a silken scarf to envelop his throat,

And his flowered waistcoat, and breeches
    blue,
And a ribbon black for the end of his queue,
And his silver buckles and gold-headed
    stick,
And his slippers thin, and his gaiters thick,

2*   21

And his powder-horn, and his musket new,
And lastly she added his field-glass too;
" Because," this provident wife quoth she,
" In foreign lands there is much to see!"

Then she sped through the village and over
    the road,
While far in the distance the Dominie strode,
And to every one questioning thus cried she,
" *The Dominie says he is going to sea!* "

So straightway the Innkeeper after her ran,
And so did the Beadle and Penny-bun Man,
The Piper and Fiddler, still playing a jig,
And the Clerk with his pen and his gown
    and his wig,

The Doctor, a-riding his old gray nag,
Came jogging along with his saddle-bag
And the Miller, too, stopped his wheel and
    he sped
With his dusty hat on his floury head;

So they went round the hill by the winding
    road,
While out of their sight the Dominie strode,
For they said, "We will meet where the
    path leads down,
And he takes the highway for yonder town!"

And to every one questioning thus cried they,
" *The Dominie 's going to sea, this day!*"
Till all with important excitement rife
Went hurrying after the Dominie's wife.

But though they scrambled and though they
    ran —
To the path where the broad highway began,
There was not a sign of Dominie Brown
On the way which led to the seaport town!

They waited and wondered and shaded their
    eyes
Till the sun lay low in the western skies;
Then every one said it was easy to see
That so notably wise a man as he,

While, after each one there hurried his wife,
All of them running as if for life,
Exclaiming, "If Dominie 's going to sea,
He has much of importance to say to *me!*"

23

Taking a voyage as sudden as strange
To give his loftiest ideas range,
Would choose his own road, and even now
Was doubtless a-sail at some brave ship's
    prow!

So back as they came, with wonderment rife,
They followed the Dominie's provident wife
Bewailing a husband who traveled like that
In his every-day coat and his garden hat!

Back where the Dominie's lands begun
They bore her company every one,
Condoling her care and her desolate state,
Till they came in sight of her garden gate.

And there, serenely shading his eyes,
With a questioning look of pleased surprise,
Stood Dominie Brown for all to see.
" Now welcome to you, kind friends!" quoth he.

" So fine a season it is for a stroll,
I too have refreshed my body and soul,
And have been to see "— he nodded his head
To the hill round which they late had sped—

" To see if yon path, if I followed it straight,
Would bring me around to my garden gate.
And it did!" The Dominie nodded and smiled,
While contentment shone in his blue eyes mild.

But nobody smiled and nobody stirred;
Only the Dominie's wife was heard,
Her eyes they flashed and she spake most true —
" *One never knows what such a man will do!*"

What things befell the Squire's House all on a Friday Morning

WHAT THINGS BEFELL THE SQVIRE'S HOVSE ALL ON A FRIDAY MORNING

"Out! Mother Meg, come out, come out,
  And hearken what I say!
There are strange happenings about
  The Squire's house this day!
The mare is gone from out her stall,—
  Alack, unlucky fate!—
Three crows did fly around the hall
  As I ran out the gate!

"A bumblebee hath stung the Squire;
  His face is twice its size.
My cake hath vanished off the fire,

Bewitched from 'neath my eyes!
Old Goody Gay doth sore bemoan
  Some spirit in the well,
Which makes the bucket weigh ten stone
  And keeps it under spell!"

Then Buxom Bess, the Squire's maid,
  Wrung her two hands, forlorning;
But simple Jake, who after sped,
Just stood and looked and nagged his head,
  All on this Friday Morning.

27

So Mother Meg a charm
    did brew
  For Bess, the Squire's
    lass:
A wondrous potion to
    undo
  What things had come
    to pass.
She drew three hairs, and
    each one named,
  From out her old cat's
    back,
And cast them in the fire
    that flamed
  Beneath her caldron
    black.

Took herbs which grew the well beside,
  Each with its magic art,
A snake-tooth and a horsehair tied,
  And earth a seventh part,
And these did brew and brew and brew,
  Within the caldron there,
    Then with her hazel rod she drew
    Three circles in the air:

"Abra-cad-abra, cad-abra, ca-di!
  Come, my cat with the gleaming
    eye,
  Abra-cad-abra, cad-abra, cad-
    ay!
    Banish spell in this smoke
    away!"

With this strange charm
    went Bess the maid
  Backward, and slow
    retreating;
And three times around
    the house she
    strayed,
And here and there the
    potion laid,
Those mystic words re-
    peating.

And lo! before the morrow, Jake
  Had caught that wandering mare;
And slyly from the well did take
  The stones he emptied there!
Old Goody, so rejoiced was she,
  Drew water till nigh spent;
Then straightway o'er a cup o' tea
  To tell her Gossip went.

No bees did sting the Squire, because
  The bees he went not nigh.
And Buxom Bess so busy was
  She saw no black crows fly.
But her good cake was gone, in truth;
  Yet this thing I do say,
She lost not one again, forsooth,
  Until next baking-day!

Now, if such signs should come to you,
  Speed straight away, I beg,
And get a magic potion, too,
  Brewed by old Mother Meg.
But of one Jake, with shambling
    tread,

Ask not the road. Take warning!
For when these things were done and
    said,
    He just stood by and wag-
      ged his head —
    All on that Friday Morn-
      ing!

The Scribe of Durley

The Scribe of Durley

SAID the dauntless Scribe of Durley, "I
    shall hie me forth to see
The midnight raiders who molest my favorite
    plum-tree.
Yestreen I counted thirty plums a-ripening
    in all;
This evening only twenty-nine are hanging
    on the wall!

"I 'll fright the bold marauders forever from
    the scene,
For tales of blood and daring my daily food
    have been.
My grandsire was a warrior who fought by
    sea and land:
I 'll sally out upon the field, his weapons
    in my hand!"

This dauntless Scribe of Durley—toward his favorite
plum-tree ;
And the gruesome armor's rusty
greaves they rattled as
he trod,
And the dint-
ed hel-
met sway-
ed and
bent with
spectral
beck and
nod.

He crawled
within the
shadows
dark, and
clambered
up the wall,
When lo! upon the
further side uprose a figure tall —
A fearful, ghostly figure, with
hairy visage black!
And the dauntless Scribe of Durley
from off the wall
fell back.

So that dauntless Scribe of Durley, when
the night was dark and still,
And the trees were black and spectral, and
the moon hung o'er the hill,
His project hazardous he hid from his
maiden daughters three,
But made him ready to protect his favorite
plum-tree.

"I 'll don my grandsire's armor," quoth he
unto himself;
"And with his shield and helmet, his long
sword from the shelf,
I 'll impress these poor marauders, when I
conquer face to face,
That they 're honored in encountering a
very ancient race !"

It was a black and gloomy way, and stealth-
ily stole he —

Forgot was grandsire's valor, as
straightway to the ground
He rolled with creak and jangle, with weird
and awful sound.
Up through that gloomy garden-close the Scribe
of Durley fled;
Dropped armor, shield and long sword, and the
helmet from his head.

And lo! upon his threshold, trembling and
panting. he —
The dauntless Scribe of Durley — met his
pretty daughters three.
One had a lighted candle, and one the
snuffers bore,
And one a gruesome cobweb-brush held
valiantly before.

" Oh, father, you are come too late!" cried
One and Two and Three;
" For armèd men this night besieged your
favorite plum-tree!

34

We heard them stealing stealth-
    ily, and followed, one and all,
With our long broom made ready to
    sweep them from the wall!

And when their leader rose on high with rattling, warlike sound,
We lifted yonder cobweb-broom and felled him to the ground!

And not a plum molested is, upon your favorite tree,
For twenty-nine a-ripening are, and one we ate for tea!"

Then the dauntless Scribe of Durley, oh, ne'er a word
   said he
About the bold old ancestor who fought by land and
   sea.
Nay, he patted condescendingly each
   pretty daughter's head,
And with candle — and with dignity —
   betook himself to bed.

The Highwayman of Durley

The Highwayman of Durley

THE Durley Coach came rattling down the steep and slippery road,
With geese and chickens swung atop, and hampers full — a load.
 "*Toot - toot!   Toot - toot!*" the coacher's
horn echoed without, within, sirs,
And said: "*Light up, light up the
fires in good old Durley Inn,
sirs!*"

And Mistress Pynch
with sampler, and with
jar of honey clear,
Sat by the Innkeeper and
wife and all their children dear;
With pickles, pie, and bird-cage, Mistress
Merrivein was there,—
For all were bringing home their goods
from distant Durley Fair.

The Durley Coach held passengers well-
nigh a half a score:
The Dominie, he sat behind; the Beadle
sat before;
And Master Mynce was packed therein,
his viol by his knees;
While Granny Gryce held sunshade green,
and half a keg of cheese;

"Stop, there!" The horses reared and plunged
   and halted in the dark.
A hand had grasped the leader's rein, and
   swung a lantern's spark.
And Mistress Pynch shrieked, "*Highway-
   men!*" with all her might and main,
And "*Highwaymen!*" screamed Granny
   Gryce and Mistress Merrivein.

"Thieves! Robbers!"
    bawled the Beadle.
    "Fling everything outside!"
"Take all we have, but spare our
    lives!" the Innkeeper he cried.
"Here is my viol," wailed Master Mynce;
    "'t is worth a pound to you, sirs!"
"My snuff-box," cried the Dominie, "and
    best umbrella, too, sirs!"

"Alack!" sobbed Mistress Merrivein, "kind
    sirs, oh, let me go!

My husband dear will pay you well, good
    gentlemen, I know!
A finer man you'll never meet, nor see his
    like again;
No one was ever yet afraid of Master
    Merrivein!"

The voices shrieked; the traps flew out,
  a queer and motley horde,
The Highwayman he shouted, "*Stop!*" The
  Coacher, too, he roared;
Came sampler, viol, sunshade, and bird-
  cage, pickles, cheese,
Umbrella, honey, snuff-box, for that High-
  wayman to seize.

The Highwayman his lantern swung, and
  chattels strove to miss.
"Alackaday, good friends," he cried, "a
  pretty welcome this!
'T is dark, and I 've a sack of grain I
  fetched from Durley Mill;
I stopped the coach to get a ride — all
  with a right good will:
But if there be no room within,— and that,
  methinks, is plain,—

I 'll climb atop." So spake the voice of
  Master Merrivein!

Then Innkeeper and Dominie and Beadle,
  one and all,
Climbed out to seek their scattered goods,
  and not a sound let fall.
But Mistress Merrivein outside the window
  stretched her head,
And to her husband dear straightway these
  were the words she said:

"In all of Durley, round about, there is not
  such a man
For making fuss and trouble! Explain it,
  if you can.
Instead of all this bother and worry and
  to-do, sir,
Why could you not have said at first that
  you were only *you, sir?*"

The Happy Thought of Mistress Pynch

Mistress Pynch's Happy Thought

QUOTH Mistress Pynch
unto her cat (a prim old
lady, she!):
"If Durley Town held no
small boys, how happy we
should be!
Young lads so unexpected are; their
manners so alarming.
I 'd work a transformation satisfactory
and charming.

"I 'd have our grown-up townsmen
grave, for space of one brief day,
Assume the guise of boyhood days,
and show us youth at play,
So circumspect! Such dignity! At
lessons late and early!
Alack, what models they would be
unto these lads of Durley!

"The Dominie — right certain I that
never in his life
Was that staid mind on pleasure bent, with
noisy pastime rife;
Our good friend Master Merrivein — so
conscientious ever!
I 'm sure that
in his boy-
hood he de-
sired a play-
time never.

"Our wise adviser, Doctor Patch — how
studious was he!
And Cousin Mynce, who always walked
abroad with sisters three!
Alas! their tasks were play enough; all
lighter pastime spurning,
They kept them to their copy-books, or
Rule of Three a-learning.

46

"Now, could these stately friends
    recall how discreetly they have
    played
In the good old days when duty the part
    of youth was made!
My cat could walk abroad in peace; in
    quiet late and early
We 'd live—if such a spell were wrought
    within the town of Durley!"

And now, of ways and
    means and things,
    don't question me. I
    beg,
(Mayhap that guileless cat
    slipped out and told
    Wise Woman Meg);
But scarce had Mistress
    Pynch so wished (a-
    nodding o'er her fire)
Than came a sound down
    Durley Hill, a-mount-
    ing high and higher!

In consternation, Mis-
    tress Pynch
    sprang up and
    to her door.
Lo! such a sight
    there met her
    eyes as ne'er
    they 'd seen
    before!

A shout! A roar! Stampede and dust!
   Down Durley Hill came rushing,
Like to a living torrent or a long-pent flood a-gushing,

A medley of the queerest folk, with whistles, yells, and noise;
Now, were they young, or were they old, these savage Durley boys?
   Upon good Mistress Pynch's cow the Dominie came riding,
   While hanging to old Dobbin's tail fled Doctor Patch a-striding!

The Beadle? Down the hill, head first, he made a
   mighty start, sirs,
And after came the ponderous Squire upon a baby's
   cart, sirs!
   While Cousin Mynce (O lackaday, that I
     should do the telling!)
   Was tying tins unto the cat, regardless of
     its yelling.

And gentle Master Merrivein (it well-nigh
   makes me quail!)
Came pounding out a wild tattoo on Mis-
   tress Pynch's pail.
   The fences fell; the gates flew off; the
     signs were madly swinging;
   Books whirled, and dogs they barked like
     mad, and cow-bells all were ringing;

48

Big stones they flew the casements through; the drums all
   beat, the whistles blew;
Oh, such a havoc, racket, din! The glass clashed out;
   the folks dashed in!
To tell the half I can't begin. The very earth began
   to spin
Round Mistress Pynch, when these old boys shouted, with
   savage dance, sirs:
"This is the very way, oho! we should have played long,
   long ago
In the good old days of youth, you know — *if we 'd only
   had the chance, sirs !* "

*   *   *

Poor Mistress Pynch! She wrung her hands — and then she rubbed
   her eyes;
For she sat before her fire, while her cat, with meekest guise,
Was licking of its two black paws. The sunset
   red was falling,
And somewhere near, on Durley Hill, the
   boys at play were calling.

Then Mistress Pynch she got her up
   and peeped without her door;
And straightway from her pantry all
   her gingernuts she bore,
And carried them — ay, every one —
   so spicy, crisp, and curly,
   ('Mid great astonishment and
   awe), unto those lads of
   Durley.

The Enviable Errand of Master Merrivein

The Enviable Errand of Master Merrivein

QUOTH Mistress Merrivein, one morn, "Go! Get ye forth right early,
And fetch a pound o' tea from out the market-place o' Durley;
Of green alpaca buy a yard, red ribbon for my muff,
An earthen crock, a skein of yarn, ha'penny worth o' snuff,
    A wooden pail, a pair of mitts, and flour from the mill, sir;
    And, that you may return full soon, go round by Hyburn Hill, sir."

So kindly Master Merrivein, he hied him forth right early;
And this is what he told himself upon the road to Durley:
"Of red alpaca buy a pound, a pail of tea, a muff;
    Green mitts, a skein of flour, and a half a yard of snuff!"

And as he went down Hyburn Hill, a-whistling blithe and cheery,
He met the market-woman, who came out from County Kerry,
    With basket balanced on her head, and panniers at her
      side,
    She bobbed to Master Merrivein; and this was what
      she cried:

"Arrah, now, pretty gintleman! Coom,
    sthop awhile an' buy!
I 've spectacles to match the rogue
    a-twinklin' in yer eye!
Wid neckerchiefs an' finger-rings — most
    beauchiful they 're shinin'!
To suit ye dacintly an' grand, I 'll
    sthraightway be divinin'."

But Master Merrivein, the wise,
    he sagely shook his head,
And to the market-woman these
    mysterious words he said:
"Of red alpaca buy a pound;
    a yard of mitts and muff;
Green flour in a wooden crock,
    and half a skein of snuff—"

"Begone!" that market-woman
    cried; "the likes of ye
    should know
A dacint market-woman 'll not be
    tr'ated so!"

Down Hyburn Hill she followed him,
    with hard and furious pace,
        Till nigh the hurrying throng outside
        the Durley market-place.

And there, with her black cat. was Meg, the Witch o' Durley Green.
"Hold, now, and hearken, sir," cried she; "your fortune I have seen!
Strange stores indeed of gold and gear this day are waiting you;
But he who 'd find aright must buy my magic snake-tooth brew!"

But Master Merrivein the wise, he
sagely shook his head,
And to the Witch o' Durley Green these
mystic words he said:
"Of red alpaca buy a skein — a crock of
muffs and things;
Green spectacles, a pail of snuff, a pound
of finger-rings — "

"Hoots! Toots!" the Witch o' Durley cried,
'mid shouts and gibes and laughter,
As with her stick upraised in air she angrily sped after.
While Jake the Pieman, ran before, a-calling "Cake or tart, sir?"
And Moll, the gypsy, ran beside, a-crying, "Make you smart, sir,

"With laces, ribbons, yellow beads, and little looking-glasses!
An' you'll be finer than the lads, an' fairer than the lasses!"
But with his hands upon his ears good Merrivein, he sped,
While they followed, in amazement at the queer words that he said.

"Of red alpaca buy a crock, a pail of rings, green muff;
A half a pound of spectacles, a yard of snake-tooth snuff"—
Oh, then he fled beyond their shouts, that nobody might
     find him;
But buxom Bess, the squire's maid, went running on
     behind him.

And Polly from the Ferrier's, and Peggy from the hillside,
And little Norah of Dunblea, and Nelly of the millside;
And so they ran, and oh, they ran! a-joining hands together,
Twixt Durley Hill and Durley Green, all in the windy weather.
And there,— good Master Merrivein! — upon a stone they found him;
And oh, they glanced, and oh, they pranced, and oh, they danced
     around him!
     And Polly showed a crimson shoe,
     And Norah's saucy eyes were blue,
And Bess she wore a kerchief red, and Peggy had a yellow head,
And Nelly like a lark did sing, as round they whirled them in a ring.

But through the song and laughter, and
the tripping dance so gay,
They heard good Master Merrivein's dis-
jointed utterance say:
" 'T was red alpaca in a pail . . . a pound of looking-glasses . . .
Blue muffs and things . . . red finger-rings for little dancing-lasses . . .
A skein of yellow beads and lace . . . a yard of snake-tooth tea . . ."
Alack, poor Master Merrivein, in sorry plight was he!

Then mad they danced up Durley Hill, a-flitting back together
Like butterflies, all in the glad and golden Durley weather.

But what good Master Merrivein fetched home that morning early —
Go ask of Mistress Merrivein, on t' other side of Durley!

The Battle of Durley

The Battle of Durley

QUOTH Master Merrivein, one morn, unto his wife: "I hear
The mill on Durley River bank hath been besieged, my dear—"
"Besieged!" cried Mistress Merrivein. "What news! Oh, lack-a-day!"
And off she flew to tell the news to Mistress Dolly Gay.

Meanwhile, good Master Merrivein, with not a care or frown,

Whistling, had packed his market-cart and started off for town.
But nigh half-way, a-gallop, came the doctor and his nag;
And, hard behind, the donkey-cart of good Dame Featherbag.

Lo! at the crooked turnstile, a-running as for life,
The fiddler and the blacksmith, the dominie and wife;

A-followed
by the
shrimp-man,
who, panting,
breathless, said:
"There 's fighting up at Durley Town, and
much blood hath been shed!"

And on the yellow highway he met with
sailors three,
A-hobbling up to Durley Town, as hard as
hard could be.
They carried sticks and bludgeons, and as
they passed they said:
"There 's a battle up at Durley, and sixteen
men are dead!"

Upon the bridge the innkeeper was driv-
ing like the wind,
And all his family in a cart were coming
on behind;
And they flourished warlike implements, all
threatening to strike —

Long skewers,
tongs, brass
candlesticks,
and snuffers,
and the like.

59

And out upon the highway — the strangest
  sight, I ween ! —
A throng of frightened village folk a-march
  from Durley Green,
Equipped with ancient musketry — arrayed
  from toe to crown —
To battle for their neighbors at beleaguered
  Durley Town.

And they shouted as they hastened by, each
  with a right good will:
" The soldiers are upon us, and they 've fired
  Durley Mill ! "
    And lastly came the cannon, with the
    beadle on before ;
    And he shouted, " Haste and help us,
    for there 's going to be a WAR ! "

So away went Master Merrivein, and followed them all down
To fight for suffering neighbors at beleaguered Durley Town.
But lo! what sight did meet his eyes as he drove round
   the hill?
All peacefully against the skies stood good old Durley Mill!

And thick about it there was drawn a
   strange and motley crew,
A-talking and a-clamoring, and making a
   to-do
Around the startled miller, who, with coun-
   tenance benign,
Of enemy or bloodshed had seen nor trace
   nor sign!

And lo! on Master Merrivein they turned,
   as he drew nigh,
And his wife advanced with wrathful mien
   and anger-flashing eye:
"What is this thing you 've done, sir! What
   do you mean, I say,
By telling me that Durley Mill hath been
   besieged this day?"

"Ay, ay!" cried all the neighbors, and the beadle wagged his head.
"Explain, sir! Ay, explain, sir!" right furiously he said.
  And kindly Master Merrivein, full wondering, spake he,

While all the birds round Durley Hill listened in every tree:
"I *tried* to tell my wife, good friends,—mayhap she 'll make it plain,—
  That Durley Mill 's besieged *by mice!*" quoth Master Merrivein.

White Marie

WHITE MARIE

OH, White Marie from the mountain high
Came down, when the world went Maying,
From the snow of the peaks that shine alway,
To the snow of the fields that flowering lay,
Where Shy Suzette and Saucy Dinette
— and Baby Babette — were playing.

❀

Stole White Marie from the mountain high
Like a wandering wind-flower straying;
And oh, the surprise in her soft dark eyes
At the blossoming ball of wonderful size
With which Suzette and Saucy Dinette
— and Baby Babette — were playing!

❀

Then —
Shy Suzette would not go nigh,
And naughty Dinette drew her face awry,
And frightened Marie turned swift to fly
Back to her goats, the foot-path by,
When —
Baby Babette in the grasses high —
A Marguerite out-swaying —
Reached her hands with a laugh of delight,
And scattered a shower of sunflakes white,
With nods and smiles and baby wiles,
And baby words soft saying.

64

Then!

Dinette threw her ball and cried "*Ici!*"
And Suzette looked sorry and said "*O oui!*"
And Marie murmured a sweet "*Merci!*"
　　　And then — and then —
Dear Baby Babette and Shy Suzette and Saucy Dinette,
With White Marie from the mountain high,
　　　In the snow of the fields were playing!

Lisbeth's Song

Lisbeth's Song

"WHIRR!" says the little wheel. "Whirr! Whirr!"
While out of the window a twitter and stir,
And the bells of the garden are all a-chime
With the clock in the corner that ticks the time
Solemn o'er Lisbeth's white-capped head,
And kerchief demure, and petticoat red;

"Whirr!" says the little wheel, "let me be!"
But Lisbeth laughs, and blithe sings she:
   "Soft and bright,
   Smooth and white,
    Keeps the thread in beginning,
   And I 'll have no spot,
   Or tangled knot,
    At the close of this day's spinning."

"Burr!" says the little wheel. "Bur-r-r—"
While the buds in the window beckon to her.
And the sunlight mocks at the clock's stern face,
And the big blue tiles in the chimney-place,
And dances in glee on the white floor bare,
And Lisbeth's braids of yellow hair—
"Burr!" says the little wheel, "don't you see?"
But Lisbeth laughs, and blithe sings she:
   "Turn and spin,
   Out and in,
    No end without a beginning;
   I must have no spot,
   Or tangled knot,
    At the close of this day's spinning!"

By Hook or by Crook

By Hook or By Crook

IT was a lonely Shepherd
lad, who lolled upon
the lea,—
" Alack, how many fishes
are a-swimming in the
sea !
'T would seem a goodly company were
I in yonder boat,
But here are only grazing sheep, or else
a gruesome goat !

"The sun comes up, the sun goes down, alike day after day;
I come and go with my slow sheep in just the selfsame way.
I am tired of the hilltop, I am tired of the lea,
And I would I were yon Fisherman a-skimming o'er the sea!"

It was a lonely Fisherman, who drifted with his boat,—
"Alack ! this life is nothing more than fish, and row, and float;
There 's plenty worth the living for if I were on the land,
But here the world is all made up of water, salt, and sand.

"There might be more variety if things were turned around,
And sheep went scampering in the sea and fishes on dry ground;
I am tired of the fishes, I am tired of the sea,
And I would I were yon Shepherd lad, a-lolling on the lea!"

Then the Fisherman he shouldered his basket, rod, and hook,
While the Shepherd sauntered surlily, a-slinging of his crook ;
They nodded to each other,— a nod unreconciled,—
And the great sun gave a parting look, then smiled, and smiled, and smiled!

The Fool and the Little Court Lady

THE FOOL
AND
THE LITTLE COURT LADY

He was a merry, merry Fool so gay,
  She was a little Court Lady;
He jangled his bells by night and by day,
  She sang in the green ways shady.

She sang to the Queen with the sad, sad face,
Who sighed, "Ah me!" as she listened,
"My crown for a day of such childhood's grace!"
And a tear in her dark eye glistened.

And the grave King looked at his jester gay,
And sighed, as he smiled at the chaffing.
"My kingdom to be this Fool for a day,
Whose life is a time for laughing!"

They met when the sun slipped down in the sea,
The Fool and the little Court Lady,
And a queer jester he, and a sorry singer she,
As they walked in the green ways shady;

For " I would I were the King ! " this queer Fool
    said ;
" I am tired of my jesting and my laughter ! "
" And oh, to be the Queen ! " cried this weary little
    maid,
  " And to wear a gorgeous robe forever after ! "

Then he bobbed a little bow, and a little curtsey she,
    As they passed down the green ways shady ;
But " Alack ! " quoth the queer little Fool, quoth he ;
    And " Alas ! " sighed the little Court Lady.

The Ballad of the Maid and the King

THE BALLAD OF THE MAID AND THE KING

(As told by the old Spinner.)

THE king and his men to the castle came;
    Turn, my wheel, turn!
The sun was setting, in blood-like flame;
    Turn, my wheel, turn!
The flags o' the tower were red to the west,
The dove i' the turret had sought its nest,
And I did 'broider a silken vest —
    Turn, my wheel, turn!

Clanged the horseshoe and rang the spur
    In courtyard and hall;
Owls flew forth with hoot and whir
    From the tower wall;
And out by the moat they frightened ran,
Warder and scullion, maid and
    man —
    Fled they all.

Only I in the tower was
    left —
A maid, half-grown.
My lord of his household
    all bereft —
    Hearts of stone!
My good, gray lord was
    hiding there;
Only his little maid knew
    where
    He lurked alone.

30

Strode the king to the tower door —
　　"Open here!"
Fell my 'broidery down to the floor.
　　Loud and clear,
Men in mail smote the tower wall;
Burst the door, and the king stood tall,
　　With helm and spear.

Swarmed his men up the narrow
　　stair,
　　Soldier and knight.
Found only a maiden with
　　yellow hair,
　　And a face milk-white —
Only a maid (and
　　that maid I) —
Spears and helmets
　　they thronged
　　them nigh
　　In the sun's red
　　light.

"Now who is this
　　who hath stayed
　　alone?"
　　Spake the king to
　　the maid.
"Warder o' castle and
　　keeper o' stone!"
　　'T was thus she
　　said.
"All men's places
　　I 'm left to fill —
Soldier and scullion,
　　too, an ye will —
For all are fled!"

Oh, then the laughter
　　rose harsh and
　　loud;
And words they buzzed like bees in a cloud!
But I marked the great king's angry eye,
Which sought where my good, gray lord
　　might lie.

"Where is thy lord?" quoth the king to
　　the maid;
"Point the place, or thou 'lt lose thy head!"
"My life may be thine," said the maid to
　　the king;

"But my lord's is his own!" quoth she,
　　court'sying.

"Lead thou on to his hiding-place,
　Or I burn the castle before thy face!
　I level the castle from turret to ground
　Unless thy lord be straightway found!"
　　　　　Cried the king to the maid.

She stamped her foot on the pavement
　　stone —
　　She defied the King.
"Wouldst threaten a maiden left alone?"
　　How scorn can sting!

"A captive thou in a dungeon low,"
　　Said the king to the maid,
"Unless his hiding-place thou 'lt show,
　　Where he lurks in dread!"

Spake the maid: "The great king I obey!
Mine be my life! I shall lead the way
To where my lord hath hid him this
    day!"
        These words she said.

"Bravely pledged! An' thou 'lt play me true!
Or thy life is the price, and the deed thou 'lt
    rue,
        I vow to thee!"
        Oh, stern spake he.

"If I show not where he is hid this day,
My life is the forfeit that I shall pay!"
        And thus spake she.

Forth from the castle, with clamor and
    speed,
        Rode the king and his men;
One in advance on a fiery steed,

Urging me onward to point the way
To where my dear lord, good and gray,
Had striven to save his life that day.
        Then, oh, then
They rode abreast and they rode in state
        At a maiden's word;
Out by the courtyard and castle gate,
        Where swallows whirred;
Up the highway and over the hill,
Past the river, with desperate will,
        Was our galloping heard.

Into the forest, and dusk at last
        Fell quick, so quick!
The dead leaves swept in a cloud as we
    passed,
        Thick, so thick!
The dark crept round like a smoky shroud;
The horses they panted hard and loud —
"If thou play false," said the king, "beware!"

82

" 'T is well," said she of the flaxen hair;
" If I lead not where he hath hid this day
My life is the forfeit, an' that I 'll pay ! "

Over the river and past the moat,
Drawbridge, ferry, and lagging boat;
Swift they unhorsed them, each and all,
And stood without a turreted wall.
Through the postern, soldier and knight,
Blades made ready and torches alight,

Listen ! Only a maid was there,
Flitting before them up the stair —
The selfsame stair they had trodden o'er,
The selfsame castle they 'd searched before:
    Listen ! Oh, listen !

How that maiden laughed as she upward
    sped
To the empty tower room o'erhead !
But the king he shouted in baffled rage,

Following whither that maiden bid,
To where her good, gray lord was hid.

Within those portals,—silence all,
Torches wavered on cornice and hall.

And they trembled — soldier, knight, and
    page,
        But not the maid.
She sprang to the room in the turret high,
And faced them all with a flashing eye;

83

And the torches flamed: but she laughed
    the more
At an upturned stone in the pavèd floor—
At a stairway dark and steep and low,
Where into the depths a man might go.

"Behold my dear lord's hiding-place!"
      Cried the maid to the king.
"I led thee to 't with a right good grace,"
      Quoth she, court'sying.
"Thou didst leave him hiding beneath this
    stone;
And now my lord is away and gone!
Thou didst go by the courtyard and come
    by the moat;
Thou didst go in the saddle and come by
    the boat;
Thou hast been all round my lord's domain,—
Round his castle and back again.—
And he fled when ye left him — my good,
    gray lord!
And my life I yield to the great king's
    sword!"
      Said the maid to the king.

"And by my sword thou shalt straightway die!"
      Spake the king to the maid.
"Strike!" I cried (for the maid was I —
A slip of a girl, with yellow hair).
Flashed his furious blade in air,—
But lo! what a protest burst anigh!
All his knights with their swords on high!

Every soldier with flaming eye!
Blades flashed bright in the torches' glare,
A protecting ring o'er that maiden there!
No tyrant's sword could pierce that wall —
Not one drop of her blood might fall!

Beyond the yawning portal-stone
The great king stood, and he stood alone,
With never a man to call his own;
Gazing, amazed, at the swords held high
O'er a slip of a maid —
      And that maid I!

I sit and I spin in my tower room;
    Turn, my wheel, turn!
The year blows in with the apple-bloom;
    Turn, my wheel, turn!
But listen! When, wailing, the year fades
    out,
And dead, dry leaves they whirl them
    about,
And the sun lies red on the turret and wall,
    I hear once more the trumpet call;
The clamor arises, the rage, the din,
As dusk, the merciful, darkens in,
And a slim, young maid with a milk-white
    face
Rides through the night at a fearful pace —
Leads to her good lord's hiding-place —
Faces the furious king anigh:
I am old, I am old!—
    But that maid was I!

Over the Bridge to the King's Highway

Over the Bridge to the King's Highway

Over the bridge to the King's highway
  They throng and they jostle, young and old,
With bustle and with hurry; for 't is market-
    day,
  And the mist from the river riseth cold.

Over the bridge they speed, the noisy folk,
  With chaises, with barrows, and with carts;
The 'prentice in his cap, and the dame in her
    cloak,
  And the baker with his fresh-made tarts;

The friar with his book, and the jester with
    his bells,
  The vender with red apples for his stands,
The maid who buys, and the master who sells,
  And the little lass with blossoms in her hands.

Oh, the violets smile like her sweet blue
    eyes,
  As dawn on the river stealeth down;
But nobody heeds them and nobody buys,
  For 't is market-day in yonder busy town.

87

Over the bridge they have sped them one and
all,
  She watches, and she nods, and understands;
For they are so great and she so small—
  This little lass with blossoms in her
hands!

Will they stop? Nay, nay! they are grand,
they are great,
  She nods, and she smiles, and understands;
They have no time, while the court doth
yonder wait,
  For a little lass with blossoms in her hands.

Over the bridge to the King's
  highway
They are riding in the noontide
  sun,
The lords and the ladies, the courtiers gay,
  A-gleaming and a-glancing every one.

Oh, they flash and they dart past her sweet
blue eyes,
The merry, the courtly, and the sage;
She sees the lance that lights, and the feather,
too, that flies,
And the lagging of the little foot-page.

She knows how the page with his lagging lit-
tle feet
Would fain for a wee rest stay;
They have journeyed so far, they have ridden
so fleet,
The noble, the kingly, and the gay!

88

Then swiftly the leaves of her violets blue
  Are brushing his wan, pale
  face,—
Oh, my blithe little lass, the court
hath need of you,
  Of the gift, and the giver, and
  the grace !

Just a pause, just a smile from
her bonny sweet eyes—
  And the river, how it laugheth
  to the sands; .
For the tired little page like a
winged bird he flies
  A-bearing dewy blossoms in his
  hands!

Over the bridge in the noontide
bright
  They have sped like an arrow
  from its bow;
The little lass a-shading her eyes
for the sight,
  The little page's plume sweep-
  ing low.

And, oh, the river sings, not of courtier or sage —
  Nay, they haste while the great court com-
  mands;
'T is a song of the lagging of a little foot-page,
  And a little lass with blossoms in her hands.

What the Lord High Chamberlain Said

WHAT THE LORD HIGH CHAMBERLAIN SAID.

—

LITTLE Prince Carl he stole away
  From the gold-laced guard and the powdered
    page,
And the ladies in waiting. who night and day
  Kept their bird in a gilded cage.

Alone in the twilight gray and dim.
  He climbed on the carven chair of
    state,
And there with a smile sufficiently grim,
  And a royal air, His Highness sate.

" With the Dowager Duchess I shall begin;
    When I say, ' Stand forth!' she shall bow her low.
' For me to jump you have said was a sin;
    I command *you* to jump wherever you go!'

" The Court Physician I next shall take:
    ' And you, I hear, have declared it best
That I, your monarch, shall not eat cake,—
    Plum-cake, too, of the very best! —

"'Well, *you* are to eat a gallon of rice,
    And nothing besides, for every meal;

93

I am sure 't is quite " wholesome," "nourishing," "nice,"
But I know quite well just how you feel!'

"Now let the Lord Chamberlain have a care!"
His Highness' voice took a terrible ring;
He rumpled his curls of yellow hair,
And the pea-green cockatoo shook in its swing!

"'Down! Get down on your knocking knees,
Down with your smile and your snuff-box, too!'
I will thunder, 'and now 't is time, if you please,
To settle an old, old score with you!

"'What became of those three white mice
    That crept from the royal nursery door,
After you said if they did it twice
    They should never be heard of any more?

"'*I know, for I heard the little one squeak!*
    And I ran and stopped my ears up tight.
You need not squirm, and you need not speak,
    For your fate shall be settled this very night.

"'In the darkest depths of the dungeon lone
    You are to live; but do not fear,
For company livelier than your own
    You shall have three million mice a year!'"

The little Prince clapped his hands in glee,
    And laughed aloud at this fancying,—
Oh, a rare and a wonderful monarch he!—
    And the pea-green cockatoo hopped in its swing:

When out of the twilight a slow voice rolled;
    There stood the High Chamberlain, stern, who said:
"I regret to state that I've just been told
    It is time for Your Highness to go to bed!"

And lo! not a word did His Highness say!—
    He went at once, like the son of a king.
But his bright curls drooped as he walked away,
    And the cockatoo's head went under its wing.

Old Christmas

Allegretto.

It's a long way round the year, my dears, A long way round the year! I

found the frost and the flame, my dears, I found the smile and tear! I

Old Christmas.

I.

It 's a long way round the year. my dears.
A long way round the year!
I found the frost and the flame. my dears.
I found the smile and tear!

II.

The wind blew high on the pine-topp'd hill.
And cut me keen on the moor:
The heart of the stream was frozen still.
As I tapped at the miller's door.

III.

I tossed them holly in hall and cot.
And bade them right good cheer,
But stayed me not in any spot.
For I 'd traveled around the year

IV.

To bring the Christmas joy. my dears,
To your eyes so bonnie and true:
And a mistletoe bough for you. my dears.
A mistletoe bough for you!

bring the Christmas-joy, my dears, To your eyes so bonnie and true ; And a

mistle-toe bough for you, my dears, A mistle toe bough for you!

www.ingramcontent.com/pod-product-compliance
Lightning Source LLC
Chambersburg PA
CBHW030545270326
41927CB00008B/1525